Praise for Kick Start Your Success

"Do-able and inspiring! I got my dream job in three weeks by demonstrating my potential value to my company."
— Louisa Kwan, Financial Specialist

"Taking a half day to complete the book was a blessing. I now know how to utilize my creativity to make a living."
— Sherry Rickert, Work-at-Home Mom

"It's *The Kick-in-the-Pants and Achieve-It Guide.* The practical exercises gave me the confidence that I can win according to my own terms. And that I deserve it!"
— Robin Griffin, Corporate Executive

KICK START
your
SUCCESS

Four Powerful Steps to Get What You Want Out of Your Life, Career, and Business

ROMANUS WOLTER

WILEY

JOHN WILEY & SONS, INC.

Published by John Wiley & Sons, Inc., Hoboken, New Jersey.
Published simultaneously in Canada.

For general information on our other products and services or for technical support, please contact our Customer Care Department within the United States at (800) 762-2974, outside the United States at (317) 572-3993 or fax (317) 572-4002.

Wiley also publishes its books in a variety of electronic formats. Some content that appears in print may not be available in electronic books. For more information about Wiley products, visit our web site at www.wiley.com.

Library of Congress Cataloging-in-Publication Data:

Wolter, Romanus,
   Kick start your success : four powerful steps to get what you want out of
your life, career, and business / Romanus Wolter.
     p.   cm.
   Includes index.
   ISBN-13 978-0-471-77346-7 (cloth)
   ISBN-10 0-471-77346-8 (cloth)
   1. Success—Psychological aspects. 2. Success in business. 3. Attitude
(Psychology) I. Title.
   BF637.S8W66   2006
   158.1—dc22
                                2005022394

Printed in the United States of America.
10 9 8 7 6 5 4 3 2 1

To everyone who has the courage to kick start their success and change the lives of others, thank you for pursuing and sharing your dream. I look forward to being part of and hearing about your adventures and achievements.

CONTENTS

FOREWORD

How many steps does it take to shift your business and your life from ho-hum into high gear? Many people are daunted by the countless steps they must take. They are overwhelmed at the mere prospect of instituting so many changes.

But Romanus Wolter sees it differently. He sees that there are four and only four steps to take. His brilliance at seeing a complex task, then showing it to us with simplicity and clarity are what make this book mandatory reading for anyone who knows that there must be something better out there — something better than what they are settling for right now.

Best of all — Romanus shares his acumen with clarity and warmth. There is nothing preachy in these pages, but there is timeless wisdom, presented in an extremely readable manner. Rarely is a work of nonfiction a real page-turner, but you'll want to turn the pages of this book as rapidly as you can because there is enlightenment on the next page, and on each page after that.

Rather than fill your mind and these pages with words, Romanus fills them with brilliant but brief ideas—ideas that represent thousands of words. He could have used all the words, showered his readers with all the ideas, all the notions, all the tips. Instead, like a scientist, he has focused on the most important, most meaningful of these ideas, then presented and explained them to his readers.

As a result, readers can take lessons from small business success and translate them into lessons for success at life. As all thinking people know, life comes first and business comes next.

Both of these concepts—life and business—are addressed in this book. They are addressed with insights so real and so true that each one is a revelation. Rather than overfill your mind with verbiage, Romanus fills it with exactly what you need—not too much, not too little, but the exact amount you need to succeed at your life's work and to succeed at life itself.

It's really not all that simple to lead a sensible and fulfilling life, yet it is far simpler than you ever could fathom before you read this book. Truly, it is all here—the ideas, the motivation, the mind-set, and the secrets. Romanus could have titled this book *Life: A User's Manual,* but instead, he gave it the title that describes exactly what the book is about: *Kick Start Your Success.*

Consider yourself blessed to be holding in your hands the book that can literally change your life and your business for the better. Can you really do it? Yes, you can. Remember that the *Ark* was built by amateurs and that the *Titanic* was built by professionals.

Nobody can create the ideal life for you except you. And now someone has illuminated the path for you. I wish you joy as you follow it.

Jay Conrad Levinson
The Father of Guerrilla Marketing
Author, *Guerrilla Marketing* series of books
Over 14 million sold, now in 41 languages
Marin County, California

KICK START YOUR
SUCCESS: A HERO'S TALE

The mission of this book is to provide practical action steps that people can take to achieve their goals confidently. The book began, as many life-changing journeys do, with my family.

As I was growing up, my dad was my hero—straightforward, kind, and loving. From humble farm beginnings, he became a very successful international businessman. His coworkers loved him because he was a leader who helped out whenever necessary, and he never spoke negatively about anyone or anything. A hero!

Dad provided for the family without ever complaining: correcting our homework, officiating disputes with a kind resolve, and laughing at our bad jokes. My hero!

Dad was always "there" for other people. His sense of humor and smile welcomed strangers into our home. He was always willing to lend a hand without question or thought of reward. A hero!

My dad worked long hours and weekends. I remember asking him the simple question: "Dad, why do you love your job so much?"

Without taking a second to blink, my dad, my hero, looked me square in the eye and replied, "Son, I don't love what I do. I go to work to make money. I do what I love on the side."

I was shocked! What? That's impossible. The happiest person I know dislikes what he does for a living? And he hasn't had a chance to pursue his dreams!

Feeling very sad, I whispered, "That seems wrong."

My dad leaned forward and said, "That's life—it is the way the world works."

At that moment, my definition of hero changed forever because instead of agreeing with him, I replied, "Dad, you have told me over and over that I can accomplish anything I desire. What about you?"

Staring at me, my dad replied, "I've always wanted to help people build their dream products." He began volunteering time at business incubators and schools. He told others about his goal and all of the people he had helped in the past became his new support team.

My dad built his dream career and simultaneously changed my definition of hero forever. It is now "anyone who dares to take action to achieve his or her goal."

My dad is still my hero—in fact, over the next few years he continued to discuss his dreams with our family and let go of "the way it was supposed to be done." He achieved greater success then he ever imagined.

By the time you finish *Kick Start Your Success*, you will be a *hero* or *heroine* who believes in your goals and in taking action to achieve them. The path is going to be refreshingly different, so enjoy the ride!

ACKNOWLEDGMENTS

The creation of *Kick Start Your Success* was possible only through the dedicated work and support of friends, family, and colleagues. To Keith for his creative inspiration; this book and my career would not be as much fun without him. To my dear friends Dr. Joe Rubino, Robin, Marni, Sherry, Glenn, Margot, Ian, Imal, and Ellen for providing unlimited access to their passion and intellect. I express my great appreciation.

TERMS YOU SHOULD KNOW

Success develops from keeping a positive mind and attitude. A few original sayings and new definitions for common words contained in *Kick Start Your Success* include:

Community of Opportunity: The people surrounding you—friends, family, colleagues, and members of organizations to which you belong—who help you succeed by sharing contacts, ideas, and resources.

Corporatepreneurs: People who have new product and/or process ideas that will improve their present employer's business practices and profits.

Dream Like a Child, Decide As an Adult: A methodology to retain inspiration and move forward with your goals. Like a child, seek what seems impossible and ask for help. As an adult, use your intuition, experience, and knowledge to decide the next best action to take. And take it!

Experts: You are your best expert, because you know what you want to create and to what extent you will take action to make it a reality.

Fear: Contains the energy to make what *seems* impossible—possible.

Intent: The power motivating you to achieve your goal.

Grumble Buddy: The only person in the world to whom you can complain—this is the person who motivates you to stay positive and take action.

Inter"ask"ive: The ability to ask people for what you want, listen, and create a "you"nique strategy for success.

Lazy: Doing what comes to mind, rather than exploring your true motivations.

Passion: The goal you want to accomplish right now, in the moment.

Research: Taking "field trips" to explore the world and discover the answers and resources you need to succeed.

Ultimate Success: The confidence and ability to continually learn, explore, and achieve.

Note: If there is a word or activity that frightens or challenges you, give it a new definition that matches your personality, so you can successfully move forward. Please send the word and its new definition to *The Kick Start Guy* (Romanus@kickstartguy.com), and I will share it with others!

STEP ONE

Gain Confidence by Stating Your Intentions

Action: Define your goal and be motivated by your own definition of success.

Success: Building self-confidence by starting on your unique path to success.

Very few dare to strengthen the belief in themselves enough to go after their goals. This step awakens the conviction that already exists in you. Understanding your real intentions is simple and powerful.

We often put off defining and achieving our goals because we fear that if we do not follow the "way it is supposed to be done," we will fail. Good news: The world in which we live today changes very quickly. New technologies, different sales venues, and amazing jobs are created every day. Therefore, the path to achieving an objective transforms daily and, at times, hourly.

The same is true for your definition of success. It transforms as you gain knowledge. As you progress toward a goal, you learn from the real world and adjust your goal.

Once you accomplish something, you ask yourself, "Now that I achieved this, what is next?"

～～～

Life is about exploring the world so you can discover what makes you happy and success-ful *in this moment.* Continue to change and evolve. It is part of growing as a human.

～～～

Continually adjusting your goal is natural. A few weeks after you get that new job you really wanted, you will be thinking about your next promotion. The product you are developing to revolutionize the way people edu-cate their children will change as you discover how to manufacture and package it. The story you want to write will be much different when it hits the big screen or is published as a book.

Unwrap the unknown and be surprised. Acknowl-edge the fact that your goal will transform by writing *My definition of ultimate success will change as I discover how to make my goal a reality* below:

_____

_____

_____

_____

_____

Celebrate each "version" of your success. Explore your current goal and find out how to connect it to the real world. Use what you learn to REDEFINE your definition of success and take action to create your next new reality.

Life Is Full of Multiple Successes

You can have anything for yourself if you take action. It is not difficult, and it doesn't have to take a lot of time. Read the biographies of famous people and discover that they had multiple careers and successes:

- Benjamin Franklin was a writer, publisher, and then a congressman.

- Abraham Lincoln failed as a storekeeper, lost in his first attempt to obtain public office, failed when he ran for the U.S. Senate, and yet is known as one of America's greatest presidents.

- Donald Trump declared bankruptcy more than once before becoming a billionaire real estate investor, casino owner, and media darling.

- My friend's mom was a floral designer and, at the age of 44, started the process of becoming a neuroscientist. Yes, a brain scientist!

Success begins by building the right foundation. One that keeps providing you with the ideas
and inspiration you need to continue improving.

So . . . What Do You Do?

The most frequently heard question in your life may be,
"What do you do?"

Your answer to this simple question can kick start
spectacular changes in your life and work. The enthusi-
asm with which you answer this question, the words you
choose, and the confidence you project affects people's
belief in your ability to achieve goals. If you believe in
yourself, others will, too.

Most people only know what we tell them
about ourselves. Speak positively about your
current goal and people will focus on helping
you achieve it.

Every time you answer this question, you are really
creating a new beginning for yourself. This query is a perfect opportunity to tell the story of your current goal in

such a memorable way that people will want to know more. You accomplish this by focusing on the most compelling part of your answer. Describing the *how* and *why* of what you are doing, rather than just listing a title.

The outcome you want to develop is simple: To inspire other people to remember your current goal and open doors that can lead to even greater success.

Gain Personal Focus by Writing Your Intent Down

Most people speak from their minds rather than their hearts, setting them up for a rough start. When asked what their goal is, they usually respond with, "I want to find a girlfriend." "I would love to start a restaurant." "I want a job as a marketing director."

These fact-based definitions do nothing to inspire support from others. People are naturally motivated to inquire about how you expect to achieve your success rather than provide you with assistance.

The first *accomplishment* on your road to success is to understand the value you intend to deliver to others and commit it to writing. Taking this action gives you the ability to speak with greater confidence. True focus develops through combining the information found both in your heart and in your intellect.

Release your internal awareness and power by defining the benefit you offer: Your Intent. *What is intent?* It is the energy within you, burning in your soul. It is an intimate understanding of how your actions will benefit others.

It is the same process, whether your goal is huge or small—the job of your dreams, finding a great babysitter, giving team members new responsibilities, or creating a multibillion-dollar company. The path to success begins by defining your intent.

When you first write something down, it may appear insignificant, because words can never truly capture our imagination. However, with the help of others, your dream will grow beyond your wildest expectations.

If I put a seed in my hand and show it to people, they will never be able to experience its potential for beauty. No one will be able to help me grow the seed successfully until I take the first step of planting it.

Once the seed begins to sprout, people will now be on the lookout for ideas for its healthy growth. They will recommend new fertilizers and volunteer to water it when I go on vacation making it easier for my plant to thrive.

The same is true for your goal. People are inspired to help when you reveal the power behind your purpose.

Two Types of Intent

Intent is the underlying emotional foundation of your goal. It gives you the personal focus, energy, passion, and commitment you need to succeed.

~~~

Open your heart. Defining the benefit you offer gets you out of your head and into the power of your passion.

~~~

There are two types of intent: internal and external. Your internal intent shows you why achieving your goal is important to you. What do you love about it? Your internal intent connects your real-world goal to your heart. And the heart has amazing power!

Your external intent shows you how achieving your goal benefits other people—establishing a positive foundation from which to build. Whether these include your new boss, a business owner, a customer, or an expectant mom—does your goal make their work easier, save them time, enable them to realize a dream, or inspire them to take action?

~~~

Intent personalizes and humanizes your goal, motivating people to want to know more about

it. Instead of questioning how you will succeed, they will ask how they can support your
efforts.

Combined, your intents establish the foundation for
the discovery of the way to make your goal a reality. Your
intent does not have to impress other people. It simply
has to be something that is important to you. By starting
from intent, you break down any intellectual barriers you
may have built around achieving your goal.

● ● ●

*Carol wanted to teach classes on how to be a great tele-
marketer. She had investigated the market for years and
created a unique road map to increasing sales.*

*Instead of starting by having her state her goal, I asked
her to write down her external intent: How will your goal
benefit other people?*

*She simply stated, "The information will help com-
panies increase sales and remove frustration in both their
personnel and their customers."*

*She began to develop her classes and was ready to
launch when tragedy hit. Both her parents fell seriously ill,
and she had to take care of them. She called me in tears, "I
can't pursue my goal of creating the sales classes because I
can't travel out of town. I can't believe I've failed."*

I asked her, "What was your goal?" She said, "To create the sales classes . . . Wait. . . . No, looking back, my intent was to deliver expertise that streamlines the sales process. Perhaps I could focus on writing by creating a newsletter or a book."

Investigating the how and why behind her goal rather than viewing her current plan as fixed freed Carol to find other strategies to accomplish her goal. Circumstances change, but not our heart's intent.

● ● ●

For a new job, you want to discover what the company, its employees, and your new boss need to succeed. Getting personal inspires people to interview you rather than dismissing you because of your past work experience.

● ● ●

Tim worked on the development side of a television and film corporation. His dream was to move over to the production side of the business so he could be part of the real-world action of creating a show.

However, no matter how many people he spoke to or how many internal production jobs he applied for, the answer was always the same, "No one moves from development to production. The work takes different skills. And the two sides don't get along because of divergent personalities."

Tim liked his employer, but he was frustrated because he feared he would have to change companies in order to obtain his dream job. After attending one of my seminars, he decided to try a different approach.

Instead of setting his goal as "getting a job on the production side," he wrote down his intents. For his internal intent, he stated that he wanted to get into production so he could have the hands-on experience of creating a show. He wanted to see the results of his work on the air rather than merely written on a piece of paper.

His external intent was more difficult to define—as it usually is. After thinking about how others (his employer, his new boss) could benefit, he realized that he had done a great job on the development side. He worked successfully with production personnel, and he had outstanding reviews.

Wouldn't his company be able to produce a better product—a higher quality television show—if they had a person who understood both the development and production processes? Couldn't they save money by finding hidden costs? Yes!

Tim uncovered a unique benefit that he could share with his manager and other people who were hiring for production positions. As we follow his story, you will discover how his focus on positive benefit opens new conversations and opportunities.

● ● ●

Intent Is Powerful

Intent unites your goal with your passion. Other people may have goals similar to yours, but they will never be able to match the unique benefit you offer.

〰️

Passion plays a huge role in success. If you love what you do, everyone knows you will find a way to make it real.

〰️

Writing your intent down taps into your intuition and beliefs—your skeleton. It enables you to believe in yourself and your goal, which begins to produce muscle and skin. The knowledge you gain as you take action thickens your skin and your ability to withstand temporary setbacks.

〰️

You don't have to have all the answers before you begin—you just need to define the passion behind your goal so you know what you are truly trying to achieve.

〰️

It is miraculous to experience the amount of energy that is generated when you decide to open your heart and mind to what you truly want to create. By focusing on what you love about your goal, you gain confidence about the real reason you want to achieve it. You are able to let go of all the "this is what I should be doing" and get on with "this is what I want to be doing."

● ● ●

Mark had his own public relations (PR) firm and wanted a change. He just wasn't passionate about his business anymore. Creating press releases did not excite him, and he felt he was always focused on mundane tasks. However, he couldn't just quit because he had a wife and son to support.

He didn't know what else he wanted to do—start a new career or get a marketing job? Instead of sinking in the quicksand of self-doubt, he started by writing down his intentions. His internal intent stated what was in his heart: He loved talking to media contacts about his clients.

His external intent helped him quickly gain focus—he wanted to help people achieve greater business success by building bridges between the media, their large audiences, and his clients. Wow! This was it—he didn't hate PR, he just didn't like some of the services he offered as part of his business.

Using this information, he realized that to succeed he needed to stop offering services he "thought he should sell." Instead of creating press releases and publicity campaigns, he would focus on selling consulting services that helped his clients understand how to build successful relationships.

His passion was re-ignited. By gaining focus and by defining his intentions, he went from ground zero—not wanting to do PR anymore—to becoming very passionate about his future work. His definition of success expanded to include his own satisfaction with his work.

Mark teamed up with colleagues who offered the capabilities his customers needed but that he disliked delivering. His focus was developing media relationships; his partners would create press releases and campaigns. By sharing clients, he has grown his business by creating new programs based on his passion, not on the products society expects a PR agency to offer.

● ● ●

Give yourself permission to explore how to connect your intent—your passion—to the outside world. Instead of setting yourself up for failure or putting your success in the hands of others, create your own unique path to success.

● ● ●

Sarah was having trouble finding a boyfriend. She really wanted a soul mate but felt like she never had any luck with men. She kept hoping that her friends would help her meet someone, but they never did.

At dinner one night with a group of friends, Sarah was dwelling on what was missing in her life. Instead of commiserating with her, I asked her about her intent. "How will having a boyfriend benefit you? What would you love about it?"

She stated that having a boyfriend would provide her with a sounding board for her ideas and a partner with whom to explore the world of art (which she loves). She would have someone to cuddle with at night and to share her dreams and sense of adventure.

When I asked her about her external intent, Sarah said that she had never really thought about how someone would benefit from being in a relationship with her. After a minute, she looked up at me and revealed her soul, "I guess someone would benefit, because they would be in a relationship where they could explore a piece of the world they love—hopefully it would be art. And they could share in a lot of laughter and discovery."

Wow! Her friends at the table were amazed. They just thought she wanted a boyfriend because "it was her next step." One friend looked at her and said, "I get it. I know someone who is studying art in school. You could go to a museum together. Oh, what a perfect first date that would be!"

Now that Sarah has stopped making the pursuit of a boyfriend all about her, her friends can visualize the possibility that someone else could be happy being in a rela-

tionship with her. Understanding that Sarah really is ready to bring benefit to someone else's life made her friends more willing to help her.

∿∿∿

EXERCISE
Define Your Internal and External Intentions

Passion is the foundation for creating a "can do" attitude and opening a world of opportunity. Some people fear defining a single intent: DON'T. Remember, this is just the beginning of your successful life—you will have multiple goals, multiple careers, and multiple successes.

∿∿∿

When you start a new goal, you may feel isolated and frustrated. This is normal. When these feelings occur, focus on your intent, trust your instincts, and go for it. You have nothing to lose, and so much to gain by persevering.

∿∿∿

Choose the one idea right now that is most important to you. As you complete the next steps, you will discover how your ideas fit together under the "big intent" you define in this exercise.

Do not limit the exploration of your true intentions by becoming lazy. Energize your mind and answer the hard questions. If your goal is to make a lot of money, find out what that really means. Focus on how the money will affect your life or the lives of others. That way you haven't created an opportunity for failure.

● ● ●

Steven wanted to make $1 million in two years — that was his goal. I asked him, "Do you believe you can achieve it in two years?" He replied, "If I don't, then I'll set a later date. It motivates me."

I simply asked, "Does it really?"

Steven then confessed that he actually feared that he might not achieve it. However, he thought that everyone would think he was very successful if he said, "$1 million in two years." The reality is that his doubts came through when he spoke. Since he didn't believe what he was saying, no one else did either.

Instead of setting a goal of making a lot of money, he investigated his intent and decided that what he really wanted to do was create a product to help small business owners compete against major stores. Excitedly, he explained that this product, plus associated services, would launch him on the road to success.

Steven refocused the way he spoke about his goal and found that people's perception of his success was based on how he makes a difference, not on his bank account. He is developing his prototype and is on his way to generating enough revenue to continue to expand his business.

● ● ●

Complete the following exercise by writing down whatever comes into your mind and heart. Do not analyze, just write.

1. Write Your Internal Intent

Why do you want to achieve this goal? What do you love about it? How will your life change once your goal is achieved?

_____

_____

_____

_____

2. Write Your External Intent

How will achieving your goal help other people? How will it benefit the company you work for, your clients, or the world?

_____

_____

_____

_____

Draw a Heart around Your Intentions

After you have discovered and successfully written down your intentions, draw a big heart around them.

Why? *Intent is the emotional foundation for achieving your goal.* It provides the underlying core truth, the bedrock of success. Drawing a heart around your intentions, acts as a reminder of why you are starting on this new journey. Why it is worth the potential "blood, sweat, and tears." If you are having a bad day, simply pull your intent sheet out and become re-invigorated.

〰️

Your intent has infinite intelligence. Its power moves your goal forward as if pushed by an invisible hand.

〰️

Now is the time to create a new world in which you are an integral part, not just a bystander. Your job is simple: Challenge yourself, continually improve, achieve; and then achieve some more. Become an adventurer, following your dream goal as it changes and grows. Move forward with an unquenchable desire to make a difference in your life.

One of my clients shared with me, "The intent step shoves your soul into action and there is no stopping you."

Your New "28-Hour" Day

Your intentions open up a world of possibilities. Your mind and heart will explode with opportunities that you want to pursue. Choice now enters into your decision-making process. Which activities, especially personal ones, do you seek to accomplish and which do you decide to let go?

〰〰

Flexibility is a gift you can give yourself that costs you nothing and returns so much.

〰〰

You may not realize it, but you can accomplish more in one day than your parents ever imagined. What used to be linear activities and decisions—driving to work, catching up on phone messages, planning evening events—can now be completed in parallel.

You can help your kids finish their homework while instant messaging a colleague. You can check your voicemail from your car, call your mother while grocery shopping, and, with TiVo, make a 60-minute television program 42 minutes by skipping the commercials. Life has sped up!

〰〰

No matter how hard you try to keep them separate, your personal and work time will mesh

and often, collide. It is important to remember
that you are in control of your schedule.

~~~~~

However, even with this new efficiency, guilt never
takes a vacation. The pressure to do more is unrelenting.
Your friends, family, and colleagues will probably warn
you about balancing time between your personal life and
the effort you exert toward realizing your goals.

There is no magic formula for living a successful life
in *absolute balance*. There are responsibilities you can't
ignore, but organizing them into a set of manageable activities is within your power. Stay sane and succeed by
staying calm, centered, and ready to act as necessary:

- *Push guilt aside.* To achieve your goals you often have
  to struggle and make hard choices—guilt feeds off
  this energy. Give yourself the freedom to experience
  it and let it go. Your goals were formed from your intent and are worth achieving. It is normal to feel overwhelmed at times. As you progress, you will learn to
  adapt through planning, negotiating, and prioritizing.
  You will find time for your friends, family, and fun.

- *Mentally reprioritize often.* To move forward with
  ease, you want to be constantly and consistently ef-
  fective, no matter the task. Achieve success by learning to stay calm when interruptions occur. It is
  acceptable to break from *goal mode* and focus on re-

solving the cause of the interruption. Mentally book-mark where you are on the task so you can easily ma-neuver between tasks with ease and without guilt.

- *Revel in the small tasks of life.* We often get bored with routine responsibilities such as changing a dia-per. These tasks may not feel like progress on your goal but they need to be completed. Think of these tasks as helping you get closer to success and func-tioning as a human—an accomplishment of huge proportions.

- *Know you will succeed.* No matter what distractions occur, believe that you will work through them. If you feel unsure, light a fire under your purpose by asking, "What is one action I can take right now to go after my goal?" Then take it.

Gain Support of the World

Establishing a positive foundation from which to build helps us work through the hard times we encounter when pursuing a goal. To gain even greater support of your goal, write down all the ways the world will change once you achieve your goal. List any ideas that come to mind.

For instance, when Edison invented the light bulb, his goal was to create a way to light up homes in the night. He was unsuccessful over 5,000 times. Instead of looking at his attempts as failures he stated, "I've succeeded in finding 5,000 different ways that you cannot possibly build a light bulb." At his core, Edison understood the need to persevere because of the benefits his product would ultimately produce:

- There would be less crime because people could see at night.
- Factories could stay open at night and employ more people.
- Children could play safely outside.
- Baseball games could be held at night.
- People could find their way through forests.
- New industries could be established, creating more jobs.
- The United States would be viewed as a country of innovators, inspiring people to share their ideas with our scientists.
- The light bulb could be used to explore the darkness of space.

By simply listing how the world will change, you create a wonderful momentum for your idea. Now, if you are having a rough day and don't feel like moving your idea forward, you are not just giving up on achieving your goal, but you are giving up on all the wonderful benefits the world will receive!

You have the power to achieve what is in your heart. Stop looking for reasons why something didn't work and seek new paths to make your goal a reality. Enjoy stepping toward the unexpected future, and celebrate the outcomes you produce.

An awesome way for other people to understand your goal and buy into your success is for you to share this fun list with others and ask them to add to it. Who knows, one of the ideas they come up with may be your next area of success!

List a few fun ways the world will change as you achieve your goal:

1. _____

2. _____

3. _____

4. _____

5. _____

6. _____

STEP TWO

Obtain Focus by Creating Your Instant Impact Message

Action: Use your heart, which has a powerful vocabulary, to bring your purpose into focus.

Success: Capturing people's attention and support by confidently stating the benefit connected to your goal.

There is a huge divide between imagining a world in which everything you want already exists and actually creating it yourself. The next step to success is to discover a way to talk intelligently about the benefit you offer, so that others are inspired to support your efforts.

An *Instant Impact Message* is a brief, personal, powerful statement based on benefit that you consistently repeat to everyone you meet. Revealing the benefit behind your goal to the world and asking for help when you need it builds self-confidence.

≈≈≈

Trust is an intangible, valuable asset. If your message is believable and genuine, people you come into contact with will trust you immediately. This is why referrals, idea exchanges, and sales between people who have never met each other occur all the time.

～～

The goal of your Instant Impact Message is to make a *direct impression*. You want to capture the hearts and imaginations of your audience. By developing an understanding between yourself and another person based on benefit, you capture the attention you need.

New acquaintances have short attention spans, so make your Instant Impact Message less than 10 words. You may not get there the first time you write down your message; that is normal. Sharing your message with others will enable you to bring focus to your intent.

～～

Share your Instant Impact Message with others. They do not have all your baggage and will give you the perfect word that was missing from your statement.

～～

You may have heard that you have to catch other people's attention within the first 30 seconds you meet them, otherwise they will not remember you. Alternatively, you may have heard it said that because of today's fast-paced world, you have to create a great impression within the first 10 seconds of your meeting someone. I've recently read that it's actually the first 5 seconds that count most.

Less is more. Set your stage by telling people only what they need to know.

The truth is that we can't control people's subconscious impressions of us. If we dress for success, some of the attendees in the meeting will think, "Wow, they are really successful." Someone else, maybe even the boss, will believe, "They're dressing to impress me." And then, of course, there is the person who believes, "The suit intimidates me, I can't wait for this meeting to be over."

However, we *can* influence people's impression of us through the first words that come out of our mouths. By speaking from the heart and about the benefit we offer, our words can instantly stimulate the response, "I believe in you, and I am going to help you succeed."

Instant Impact Message: "Open, Says Me!"

Ali Baba said "Open Sesame," and the rocks of an impervious mountain moved to form an entrance. By using the right words when you speak about your goal, you can move your own obstacles and negative beliefs aside.

〰️

> Your words dissolve barriers and attract the people, ideas, and resources you need to succeed.

〰️

You do not have to tell people everything about your goal to get them to help you. Your Instant Impact Message allows you to become *known as someone,* so people remember you and the benefit you offer. It helps you:

- Maintain focus and achieve your goals by clarifying your purpose.
- Confidently interact with others, because you have something unique, personal, and interesting to share.
- Weed out those who are not interested in helping.
- Develop winning strategies by consistently using a message that people can understand and act on.
- Discover new resources, strategies, and people who can help you succeed.

The "Luck" of the Irish

My Mom used to call me one of the luckiest people in the world—I think it was the Irish in her. After I explained to her how hard I worked at creating what others called luck, she began saying that I was the hardest working person in the world.

You are in charge. Your family and personal contacts are factors in your success but you create your own *lucky breaks* by taking continual action. Allow your intuition to guide you toward the realization of what you need to accomplish next. It creates a dynamic wave of energy that propels your goals forward.

Your Own Instant Impact Message

When people are looking to buy a new product, hire a new person, find a date for someone, or share in a unique experience, they subconsciously ask themselves: "How will I or someone I know benefit?" They analyze this instantly—that is why it is important that people are able to immediately recognize the benefit you offer.

As you create your Instant Impact Message, you may find yourself smiling as you uncover new passions.

To inspire people to listen to your message, clearly state your benefit up front. Ask yourself: "When someone meets me, receives my brochure, reads my resume, or looks at my business card—do they understand how achieving my goal can help them?"

For instance, my Instant Impact Message is, "I am known as The Kick Start Guy. I provide action steps that close the gap between goals and success." This concise statement makes it effortless for people to refer new clients to me. "You have a goal you want to accomplish but are uncertain how to do it? You have to meet The Kick Start Guy—he can help."

Develop your Instant Impact Message from your heart, not your head. Your heart and passion have unlimited wisdom.

EXERCISE
Create Your Instant Impact Message

Think "benefit" as you create a winning, personal Instant Impact Message. During this exercise, do not worry about editing any words or ideas that come to mind. Just write everything down.

1. Choose Your First Goal

If you have multiple goals, choose the one that resonates most with your heart. Do not fret about whether or not this is your life goal. As we discussed earlier, concentrate on the goal you want to achieve right now—it is the one you are supposed to be developing.

My first goal is:

_____

_____

_____

2. Write a Paragraph or More Describing Your Goal

Be specific about what you want to achieve. What does it look like?

You have to start somewhere. Allow yourself to have fun putting words around your passion by writing down whatever comes to mind. Write your paragraph now:

_____

_____

_____

3. Write a Paragraph or More about the Unique Benefit Achieving Your Goal Will Provide to Other People, Organizations, or Companies

You can obtain specific ideas from the external intent exercise you completed in Step One: Gain Confidence by Stating Your Intentions.

_____

_____

_____

4. Circle Any Key Descriptive Words in All the Paragraphs You Just Wrote

Key words are the ones that resonate with your heart. They connect with the benefit you offer and stand out from the other words. Just circle these key words.

Write your circled key words below:

_____

_____

_____

5. Give Your Goal a Name

If you want to create a new product, make a name up right now. If you want a new relationship, that can be the name of your goal. If you want to find a new job, name the type of position. If someone says, "You know a position like that doesn't exist," your reply is, "Not yet!"

Putting a name to your goal helps you own what you want to accomplish. It awakens and empowers you to discover answers. If you don't name your goal, you lack the solid foundation that says, "This is what I am going to achieve."

Having Anxiety about Naming Your Goal Is Natural!

Success is not all about you; it comes from in-spiring other people to help. If you don't like the name you come up with—be honest. Tell people you respect that you need help developing a name for your goal and ask them for ideas. They will present wonderful words that you can use if you are willing to listen to them.

～～～

You will be surprised with the names that come springing forth. If you get stuck, try using one or more of the key words that you circled as the name for your goal.

State the name of your goal: _____

● ● ●

What Makes a Name?

Tim, who wanted to move from a development job to a production job at his company, was a little reluctant to name his goal. Didn't he have to wait until the name of a job was posted?

I shared with him that I felt that no one should wait to name his or her goal—just create a name that reflects your passion. As you work on achieving your goal, people will help you find the right opportunities. They may even create a new position that matches your goal.

Tim thought about it and named his goal: The Ultimate Production Job.

Sarah hadn't had a real date in over two years. She wanted to name her goal: Get a Date Now! I reminded her that her goal needed to be grounded in how she or someone else will benefit. As an alternative to Getting a Man, *she named her goal,* Sharing My Love of Art and Life. *Instead of seeming desperate, she now portrays the true essences of her personality.*

I did not name my business The Kick Start Guy; *a client of mine did. The name of my business was* Bringing Ideas into Action *because it reflected my passion.*

After working with a client, she looked at me and said, "Thanks for providing me with the action steps to get off my butt. You really kick started me, that is your gift!" I listened to the benefit I provided, and renamed my business The Kick Start Guy. *It has catapulted my business forward, because it makes it easy for people to understand and remember the benefit I provide.*

● ● ●

6. Create Your First Instant Impact Message

Begin by writing down the name of your goal. Then, use only your circled key words to create your message. Form the words into a short, strong statement about the benefit you will provide to others by achieving your goal. You can use connector words, such as "the," "a," and "to," but do your best to use just the key words you circled to create your statement.

Your Instant Impact Message always begins with the name of your goal. This helps people easily relate to and understand what you are trying to achieve. It may feel awkward to state the name of your goal first but this simple action creates outstanding rewards.

Your first Instant Impact Message is (Name of Goal and Message): _____

_____

_____

_____

_____

_____

_____

_____

_____

● ● ●

By completing this step, Tim, who earlier named his goal: The Ultimate Production Job, *found the confidence to go after his dream job. He had wonderful development experience and great reviews. How could he inspire other people (including his boss) to help him land a job on the production side of the business, when everyone said it was impossible?*

His circled key words were: job, quality, want to watch, produce, television, save money, and satisfied. He remembered to focus on the benefit to his employer and realized that a person who knows both development and production aspects of a television show could help his company create better programs. His Instant Impact Message came together.

The Ultimate Production Job

Helping XYZ Television produce higher quality shows people will want to watch.

● ● ●

Sarah was ready for a relationship. Her friends were tired of hearing her say, "I want a boyfriend." Her circled key words (creative, discover, boyfriend, power, art, life, together, world) allowed her to develop a positive statement that changed her attitude and kick started her friends into finding dates for her.

Sharing My Love of Art and Life

Helping someone else discover the power of the creative world.

7. Say Your Instant Impact Message Aloud as Though You Were Telling Someone about Your Goal at a Social Gathering.

Would they understand the benefit you offer? Everyone who hears your message should be motivated to find out more about your goal. If not, refine your message so it focuses on the benefit achieving your goal provides.

8. Refine Your Instant Impact Message

We often save the best for last. Try reversing your message by moving the last part of what you have written to the opening. Did the benefit you provide become clearer?

Or look over the message you have created and circle three key words within it. Then, formulate a new one-sentence Instant Impact Message using those three key words.

Your revised Instant Impact Message is (don't forget to put the name of your goal first):

_____

_____

_____

9. Work on Improving Your Message as You Take Action to Achieve Your Goal

Since words can never completely capture what is in your imagination, developing your Instant Impact Message may be challenging for you.

However, sharing it with others enables you to create a message that resonates with the world. Practice your message with people and learn from their reactions by following these three rules to live by:

1. *Speak from your passion:* Your Instant Impact Message energizes you and inspires others to help you achieve success.

2. *Listen to others:* Learn from people's reactions to your message. The questions they ask and the specific words they use will help solidify your message. Someone else will give you that *perfect word* that describes your goal and the benefit it delivers.

3. *Write it down:* Don't lose any ideas. Carry a *goal notebook* with you where you can write down the words, ideas, and contacts that people give you.

Your Own Champion

Discovering the exact words for your Instant Impact Message is difficult. Begin by developing a trust in yourself to make the right decisions based on your intuition and information you gather. Acknowledge that just as your definition of success changes, your message will transform as you accumulate new information from the world.

Your Instant Impact Message puts you on the edge of vulnerability—exposing your true pur-

pose to the world. Instead of feeling weaker, realize that you have discovered a new confident
voice that inspires people to help you learn.

Stop trying to have all the answers. Successful people
know that asking for help is the key to achieving your
goals. Recommendations and ideas that others share with
you will help you solidify your message.

Your Instant Impact Message helps create human
connections that enhance your personal power and ability
to communicate with others. By allowing others to assist
in its refinement, you tap into an ever-flowing stream of
ideas, contacts, and resources to move your goal forward.

Open your mind to the wisdom that's around you.
Continually act like a champion, maintaining a positive
attitude and drive as you develop your message and pursue your goals.

● ● ●

*Flower was working on developing a career that repre-
sented the "Do It Yourself Generation." She had held di-
verse professional jobs including self-publishing children's
books and opening a store with "no credit cards, no car,
and a bad haircut." However, when people asked what she
was trying to accomplish, her response was always vague.*

*Restless, she was still searching for a way to make
something bigger of her do-it-yourself talent, but had hit a*

wall. After an Instant Impact Message workshop, the ever-innovative Flower developed a personal, more extreme process for revealing her truth.

She gathered three friends together. Rather than repeating the message she had already developed, she asked them to describe what they felt was the impact her work had on other people. Two of her friends immediately said, "You motivate." The third thought for a couple of seconds and told her, "You make me want to exercise my own creative talents even when I feel I have none."

To her amazement, their words gave her new insight into what made her happy. She wasn't just good at making things happen, she thrived at "helping others create something out of nothing." This opened new career possibilities for her that she hadn't considered, such as consulting or leading a creative team.

Make a dramatic difference in your life by being open to new approaches. Give credibility to those who observe you every day, you never know what new truths you will uncover.

● ● ●

Welcome to Focus and Self-Confidence

Your Instant Impact Message clarifies your purpose. Your goal appears *real and achievable*. It saves you time and frustration, because now you have a core message from which to leverage your efforts.

Nothing is more powerful than developing confidence in your ability to solve problems. Your trust in yourself is the core foundation for your personal power. If you work from your instincts and passion, people will want to help and support you.

Once people believe in you, they are inspired to help you achieve even greater success. Use your Instant Impact Message constantly and repeatedly. Share it with friends, family members, and colleagues, and see how they react. As you move forward, reflect what you learn in your Instant Impact Message.

If you are serious about achieving your goal, it is *always* appropriate to talk about it.

One of my clients said the Instant Impact Message process is like *creating your own legend*. Many people go through life disliking what they do for a living and complaining about the opportunities presented to them. You have begun to live your life through your intent—providing benefit to yourself and others. People will be inspired to spread the story of your success.

STEP THREE

Find Your Voice by Using Your Success Script

Action: To start powerful conversations that catapult you forward with conviction.

Success: People enthusiastically supporting your efforts—inspired to bring into existence what you cannot accomplish alone.

This is the step where all the work you have completed comes together. Success boils down to two things: speaking passionately and taking action. The foundation to accomplishing these two items is having the ability to present yourself and your goal to others with conviction.

Your conversation is not about a relationship, it is *THE* relationship. Speak and achieve what you want.

Your Success Script allows you to articulate your goal so that others can understand what you are trying to achieve. It engages people in a conversation where they are inspired to help you explore the possibilities of:

- New ways to offer your benefit
- Venues to promote your goal
- Companies to work for
- Funding sources
- People who can help
- And much more

Your Success Script takes you from ground zero, being afraid of accomplishing your goal, to becoming very passionate about your abilities and the future you are about to create. It gives you the ability to explain the benefit associated with your goal, reveal ways it is delivered to the world, show that it works, and then ask for the appropriate help to make your goal a reality.

~~~

Finding your true voice is powerful. Many people refer to the creation of their Success Script as their first moment of true understanding.

~~~

You don't have to know how to correctly achieve your goal. Your primary job is to hold on to your vision of purpose and start conversations that open the doors to success. There are a thousand paths to achieving your dream; your mission is to discover the right one for you.

Kick Start Law of Positive Words

Always speak positively about yourself and your goals. The way you feel about yourself is reflected in the silent energy you send to others, in turn affecting how people react to you. Without realizing it, we sometimes sabotage new relationships before they even begin through negative thoughts and nervous energy.

> Do not try to impress, it limits your conviction and sabotages the energy you have created by being connected to your passion.

The real-world truth is: A positive attitude attracts and a negative one repels. You don't have to love something to be upbeat about it. Rather than letting negative feelings distract you, simply concentrate on the powerful aspects of whatever is challenging you.

Positive thinking is contagious. When someone says, "That's impossible," smile and know that if you can dream it, you can accomplish it. What's unattainable to one person is merely a challenge to someone else. Electricity, television, and personal computers are evidence of explorers who looked beyond the word "impossible."

This type of positive energy guides you toward the realization of your next goal and encourages others to support your efforts. People want to work with people who have a positive outlook because they hope some of that magnetic energy rubs off on them.

For instance, Paul loathed his job, but he enjoyed working with his coworkers. In their conversations, Paul always verbalized his frustration at never advancing within his company. After attending a Kick Start workshop, Paul realized that his conversations had created a negative reality. He changed his tune and significantly improved his life.

He learned to concentrate on the positive aspects of his job and moved the negative aspects to the background. His coworkers immediately noticed. Instead of wincing when Paul came near, they saw him as a confident, capable person and offered him the tips he needed to move forward. With dedication to a more positive outlook, he in fact did get a new job—and by speaking positively, he even liked his old job a little better!

What we do is only half the story. The rest is how we do it.

Your job is simply to make conversations come alive; the results you want will develop from these conversations.

Beginning now, speak only positively about yourself, your goal, and associated challenges. Remember, no one wants to be around or support a negative person. Think about it, do you enjoy being in contact with people who sprinkle complaints into every conversation?

～～～

The *Kick Start Law of Positive Words* works both ways: If you speak about what you want to attract, you will attract it! If you speak about what you don't want to attract, you will attract it.

～～～

Affirm your intention to speak positively by writing, *From this point forward, I will speak only positively about myself, others, and my goal,* below:

_____

_____

_____

Your Grumble Buddy: "Hello World, Where Have I Been?"

Living in the past and complaining about what the world has *done to you* builds walls around your goals. A positive attitude reveals your true self and ignites possibility. Stop hiding, and open yourself up to success.

━━

Speaking positively is like learning a new language—it takes a lot of practice to become proficient.

━━

Always speaking positively is difficult, because it is far easier to complain than it is to be upbeat. It takes time to recondition your brain to look for value rather than fault. However, faster than you believe is possible, speaking positively becomes natural.

Even the most positive, upbeat people need an outlet for frustrations. Kick start the process of speaking positively by getting a *Grumble Buddy*. This is the only person in the world to whom you can complain or speak negatively—whether something goes wrong in your day, someone crosses you, you lose a contact, a client doesn't pay you, a family member whines, or your company doesn't promote you.

━━

It doesn't matter what happens in life, you can complain *only* to your Grumble Buddy.

━━

Your Grumble Buddy can't be your best friend, husband, wife, girlfriend, parent, brother, sister, or anyone else who is especially close to you. These people are in a position to love and support you, which means they do not want to see you suffer. Therefore, they make lousy Grumble Buddys. Once you complain to them, they will try to help you find a way out of the situation rather than creating a solution to help you continue forward.

For instance, when you complain about being alone, they will set you up with anyone who is single just so you can date. If you are frightened about starting your own business, they will say, "Why don't you stay in your job until you save up enough money to live on for a year?" If you wonder about how your manager will react to your request to change jobs, they will tell you to look for opportunities at another company. No one who cares about you wants to see you suffer.

Your Grumble Buddy has to be someone on the periphery of your life. I like to tell people to choose their *friend number five*—the person who is a good friend but not your best friend. Someone who respects you and who will also tell you the truth.

Your Grumble Buddy's role is: Whenever you feel the need to complain, you contact him or her and share your strife. Instead of agreeing with you about how hard it is, he or she can only reply with: "That's nice. What are you going to do next?"

That's right—no commiseration, no suggestions, no apologies—just, "That's nice. What you are going to do next?" This question trains your brain to think positively—replacing frustration with action. Soon, when things go wrong in your life, you will subliminally ask yourself the same question and take action rather than complain.

～～～

Kick start your positive thinking through the words you utter. "I can do it!" is embedded in your subconscious.

～～～

Start on the road to speaking positively by calling your friend number five and saying:

YOU: I want to make you my Grumble Buddy.

FRIEND #5: Uh . . . What?

YOU: I am working to achieve my goal of (*Insert your Instant Impact Message here*) and it is going to be very hard. This passionate "Kick Start Guy" told me that for me to succeed, I may only speak positively about my goals.

In order to do that, I have to choose a Grumble Buddy—a person to whom I can complain when anything goes wrong. I have chosen you.

FRIEND #5: Why did you choose me?

YOU: I trust you. The cool thing is that the job isn't hard. When I call, e-mail, or stop you in the street to complain, your job is to simply say, "That's nice. What are you going to do next?"

FRIEND #5: You just want me to ask you a question? No suggestions or "You're right, that's lousy?"

YOU: To help me move forward, all you have to do is say, "That's nice, what are you going to do next?"

Positive attitude and action lead to success!

Name your Grumble Buddy: _____

_____

Speak Your Goal into Existence

It is not your goal to convince anyone that you will succeed; your goal is simply to inform the people about your goal and its associated benefits.

It is almost impossible to convince someone that you are the right person to hire or that you have a product or service he or she needs. Instead, your goal is to let people know that you have what they, or someone they know, already needs or wants. You accomplish this by keeping the answers to these three questions in mind:

1. *How will I benefit the other party?* People become personally interested and inspired to want to know more once they understand how they, an organization, or someone they know will benefit. This is why your Success Script always begins with your Instant Impact Message — stating the value that you offer to the world.

2. *How will I deliver on that specific benefit?* Putting the benefit you offer into a form that is "purchasable" or "obtainable," shows others how they can easily become part of the success you are building. This does not mean it has to have a price associated with it, but it must have intrinsic value. The delivery methods in your Success Script help you accomplish this task by putting the benefit you offer into tangible form.

3. *How can I prove it really works?* Proving that the benefit you provide works reduces the fear people have about becoming associated with your goal. Testimonials from people you have worked with and helped tend to unlock other people's rolodexes, minds, and imaginations.

Your Success Script increases your "conversational confidence" by developing answers to these three questions. By becoming more focused today than you were yesterday, you build connections, understanding, and opportunities that support your goals. If anyone needs more information, they will simply ask follow-up questions.

~~~

We often save the best information for last. Your Success Script puts the benefit you offer first so you engage your audience and have a confident conversation rather than trying to make a sale.

~~~

EXERCISE
Craft Your Success Script

Your Success Script is a page of information that allows you to control the flow of conversations and keep them moving in a positive direction. Open your mind, spirit, and heart to new opportunities by reviewing the Success Script template (see pp. 60–61). Then follow the action steps presented after the template to complete it with your own information.

~~~

You can only receive the full impact of information if your conscious mind and subconscious spirit are on *ready-to-receive* mode. Your Success Script awakens both your mind and spirit to the possibilities.

~~~

SUCCESS SCRIPT TEMPLATE

Name of Goal

_____

Your Instant Impact Message

_____

_____

_____

	Delivery Methods	_Associated Instant Impact Message_
1.	_____	_____
	_____	_____
		_____
2.	_____	_____
	_____	_____
		_____
3.	_____	_____
	_____	_____
		_____

(Line number three can be used as a research tool—list a new idea and see how people respond.)

Testimonials

Short, sweet, and each supports one of the delivery items stated previously.

_____

Name, Title, Location

_____

Name, Title, Location

Bio and Contact Information

The first sentence is your internal intent—tell everyone why you love your goal so they are inspired to help you. Then show that you will achieve success in the real world by sharing your experience and, as appropriate, your key successes.

_____

_____

_____

_____

_____

Name: _____

Phone: _____

E-mail: _____

Address: _____

1. Write the Name of Your Goal and Your Instant Impact Message at the Top of a New Piece of Paper

Start every conversation with the name of your goal and your Instant Impact Message—this reminds people of the value you provide. You may become tired of saying both of them because you may feel as if you are constantly repeating yourself. DON'T! The people to whom you are speaking do not have the knowledge you have—they have to hear your message in order to understand what you are trying to achieve.

Name of Goal

_____

_____

_____

Instant Impact Message

_____

_____

_____

2. State How You Deliver the Benefit You Offer

Beneath your Instant Impact Message, list three ways that you deliver the benefit you just stated. These _delivery_ *methods* indicate how people can purchase or obtain the benefit you offer.

For a business, list your top products in the delivery area. For job seekers, state position types for which your passion and skills are appropriate. For setting up a date, list three places you could go or activities you would complete during your time together.

The delivery method slots of your Success Script support your goal and have unlimited uses. Instead of providing a snapshot of how you are or want to deliver the benefit you offer, they can also present how your past supports your current goal. Highlighting how your experience has given you the skills you need to succeed at a new endeavor allows unexpected doors to open.

For example, to support your ability to perform in a new job, list three previous experiences and the associated skills you obtained. A computer programmer can list past projects or jobs that helped bring order and structure to a chaotic environment.

● ● ●

Laura wanted a promotion within her company. Following the rule to share her goal with other people, she told her colleagues about her aspirations and asked if they knew of any job openings.

A coworker forwarded her a job posting in his department. However, he warned her that the position was for a team leader, and they might not interview her because she did not have any direct experience in managing employees.

Laura went to work on her new Success Script. Her goal was to get the job, and her Instant Impact Message became "to enable my new team to work together and achieve its goals." She reviewed her past jobs and identified specific tasks where she led or played an important role on a team:

1. *My work at an Internet start-up taught me how to deal effectively with bright people in challenging situations.*
2. *During an accounting job at a national firm, I learned to create tracking systems to keep team projects on schedule and within budget.*
3. *In my current position, I have learned the ins and outs of what it takes to effectively communicate between departments.*

After two follow-up calls, the hiring manager agreed to meet with her. At the end of the interview, he mentioned that two other candidates, who had direct management experience, were also applying. Confidently, Laura reiterated her experience and restated how she could contribute to his team.

The next morning she received a call—the manager asked her to come for another interview. He was impressed with her explanation of her abilities and her self-assurance. He wondered if she would be interested in a dif-

ferent position within his department—a job not yet posted. Within two weeks, she received her promotion.

When you believe in and prove your abilities, others will create the possibilities you need to achieve your goals.

● ● ●

When you use your Success Script, you are not "selling to anyone." You are simply checking in with the other person to determine if she or someone she knows is interested in helping you succeed. Speak confidently about the benefit you provide and let the other person process how it can assist others.

Achieving success requires constant preparation. Focus on articulating at least three ways you can deliver your benefit. Spotlight things you would enjoy doing—by default, you eliminate ideas that are not connected to your passion. This step is magical because those goals that you thought were mutually exclusive become related under the power of your Instant Impact Message.

Your Success Script encourages interaction and creates a space for people to ask you questions about your goal. If you are uncertain of how to deliver your benefit, just make up three different ways. That's right—invent three things you would love to be doing that are connected to your passion. By listening to the responses people provide to your Success Script, you will discover how the world wants you to deliver the benefit you offer.

Listening teaches you the right words to use in your Success Script. When you speak a common language, people easily connect to what you want to achieve.

Delivery Methods

1. _____

2. _____

3. _____

● ● ●

Delivery Method Examples

Tim, who was looking for a job on the production side of television, used his Success Script to name three possible business areas to which he could contribute: managing the financial analysis of shows in production, developing production budgets and matching them to available resources, and creating systems to track and report expenses and income.

Listing these three areas rather than naming a specific position opens up the opportunity for people to recom-

mend the correct contact person, mention an open job, or even create a new position based on the value he can provide. Three weeks later, he got a job on the production side of the business.

Mark wanted to grow his public relations (PR) company based on services he enjoyed providing. Using his Success Script, he tested out new ideas. His delivery methods included the development of a specific list of appropriate media contacts, hourly consulting to help clients develop long-lasting media relationships, and a four-month Launch Your PR program that included media training, contact development, and the management of press relationships.

Simply listing these options rather than what he was "supposed to offer," his business blossomed. Within two weeks, he signed several consulting clients.

Sarah, who was looking for someone to share her passion for art, thought up wonderful ways she could deliver on her goal. She listed dream dates: visiting a new exhibit at a museum, taking a glass-blowing class, and creating a painting together. (How romantic!) These ideas helped her friends appreciate the great stuff that will happen on a date with Sarah. Suddenly, most of them had suggestions for potential dates they knew would enjoy those activities.

Serena knew that her passion and the benefit she wanted to provide were tied together by her knowledge of speaking effectively in public. She went through the exercises described earlier and formed her Instant Impact

Message: Connect Now: Helping foreign executives take the fear out of speaking English in business situations.

However, she was frustrated because she couldn't decide how to sell her passion. Instead of giving her ideas, I asked her how she would deliver her benefits. Her thoughts flowed: She could work with a university to enhance their English language programs, partner with a group of experts to develop a unique training program, or provide in-house training to large foreign corporations. The possibilities seemed endless.

She created her Success Script stating three ways she could deliver her benefit. By listening to others, she discovered that a large company was looking for an opportunity to train its executives in English-speaking skills in the United States. Three months later, she was awarded a contract valued at more than $160,000 and is now expanding the program to other countries.

● ● ●

3. Expand on the Benefit You Provide by Creating an Instant Impact Message for Each of Your Three Delivery Methods.

Create an Instant Impact Message for the ways you deliver value, so that you are ready to succinctly explain them when people ask you questions. To create your individual Instant Impact Messages, simply follow the process in Step Two: Obtain Focus by Creating Your Instant Impact Message. You can even use some of the leftover circled words from the last time you completed the exercise—they build on the main benefit you offer.

Create short, powerful Instant Impact Messages for your delivery methods:

Delivery Method	Associated Instant Impact Message
1. _____	_____
2. _____	_____
3. _____	_____

4. Show People What You Can Do, and the Opportunities Will Come Knocking!

Use testimonials from clients, bosses, coworkers, and even friends to demonstrate that you deliver on your promises. Gather testimonials from everyone you benefit in order to demonstrate the value you provide. It is okay if you volunteer at a job or were not paid for a service you provided—it is the experience and the outcome you helped generate that counts.

If you want to become an in-home chef, invite your friends over for a food tasting. If your goal is to change jobs, volunteer for a similar position at a nonprofit agency part-time or offer to help on a specific project within your company.

You can write your own testimonials. After someone says something great about your ability to deliver benefit, simply ask if you can write that up as a testimonial and pass it by him for his approval. People are honored to help and will approve or slightly change what you wrote and send it back to you. This is another way to use the leftover, circled words from the Instant Impact Message exercise in Step Two.

If someone agrees to write a great testimonial, use it! List three people you will approach for testimonials:

1. _____

2. _____

3. _____

5. Connect with Others by Sharing Your Internal Intent and Experience

When people ask us what we do, we usually answer by stating our job titles or years of experience. These facts do little to inspire others to help us. However, giving your reason for wanting to achieve your goal—your internal intent from Step One: Gain Confidence by Stating Your Intentions—does indeed inspire.

Allow others to connect to the human aspect of your goal by sharing how it will affect your life; it opens up their hearts to helping you. After telling them what you love about your goal, you can then explain the experience that has made you successful. The fact that you actually have experience to support your passion will electrify anyone listening.

If you do not have any expertise related to your passion, talk over your experience with a friend to help look at it in a different light. Your "life lessons" have prepared you to be where you are right now, and your experience will help you create the success you deserve. Find a way to connect what you have already accomplished to your passion.

For instance, Tim knew he had no experience developing television programs. However, after thinking carefully about his background, he found that he understood how much money it took to create a television show, how the corporate budget process worked, and how to raise funds for a new show. These skills were necessary for him to be successful at his new job.

Committed people change the world. Stating your true intent inspires others to share wonderful possibilities.

Create your bio by first stating your Internal Intent and then your experience:

Internal intent: _____

First area of related experience: _____

Second area of related experience: _____

Third area of related experience: _____

6. Make It Very Easy for People to Contact and Refer You

Keep frustration at a minimum by making your contact information easily available. Always provide people you meet and know with information about the benefits you offer, your goals, your testimonials, and your contact information. This makes it easy for them to refer you to others.

Create an e-mail address that relates to your goal or your personal name. You can simply go to a site that offers free e-mail (Yahoo, Hotmail) and register it.

At the end of your Success Script, include your:

Main contact number: _____

Mobile phone number: _____

Address: _____

E-mail address: _____

Web site: _____

Your Success Script Has Unlimited Uses

In the 1970s, researchers uncovered the single, most important difference between great and average salespeople. The ability to listen was the secret behind those people who created an outstanding number of sales.

To succeed with ease, become *silently smart*—simply give the name of your goal and the benefit you offer. Then be quiet and let others do the work. Provide the person to whom you are speaking time to understand and respond to your information. The few seconds you wait may feel like an eternity. However, the hidden ideas and resources you uncover are well worth the wait.

Present the rest of your script by stopping after every major piece of information you supply. Listen, learn, and inspire others to help you succeed.

A likely response to your Instant Impact Message could be, "How do you do that?" By their response, they are buying into what you have said without your having to convince them of anything. To them, it seems like you are just having a normal conversation. Albeit one that you have spent a lot of time developing.

Most people do not know anything about you or your goal until you tell them. Let every thought and every act express your belief in the benefit you provide.

〰〰〰

Your Success Script is a conversational tool that you can use when networking. It can also be used as:

- A phone script for job interviews, potential dates, or selling products and services
- An e-mail letter to prospective employers, clients, and managers
- A conversation starter when networking
- A sales brochure that highlights the benefit you offer, how the benefit is delivered, and the fact that it works in the real world
- The first page of a personal or business web site— people can just click on a delivery method to gain further information
- An opening conversation for a job interview
- The introduction of a grant proposal

Most important, your Success Script is a confidence builder. Remember the phrase, "If you dream it, you can achieve it." Your script connects your mind, heart, and imagination to your goal—allowing you to speak with confidence about it, because you know you can and will achieve it.

Your Success Script as a "Real-World" Research Tool

Your Success Script can be used to evaluate people's interest in different delivery methods. Instead of always listing the ways you actually deliver (or think you will deliver) the benefit you offer, make up a delivery method and see how people react to it. Are they interested in your new idea? Do they know anyone who can help you develop it?

The only person who has the ability to discover the answers you need to succeed is you. Take action and get on with the process of achieving your goal.

For instance, list two delivery methods you know that you want to use and put a new idea of how you can deliver your benefit in the third spot. This forces you to think constantly of new ways to deliver your unique benefit—inviting a world of possibility. Listen to the reaction of others and use the feedback you receive to:

- *Determine the best action you can take to succeed.* The idea that people respond to most often is the one on which you should concentrate your efforts. If they like it, consider taking action to implement it.

- *Discover new ways to deliver the benefit you offer.* As you stimulate people's imaginations, they will provide additional ideas on how you can achieve success. Listen to them.

- *Understand what probably won't work.* If no one is interested in one of the ways you deliver your benefit, drop it. Focusing on ideas that have the most resistance from the world can be unproductive.

~~~

"Working hard" does not have to be associated with pain or long hours. It's simply the action of applying effort to produce favorable outcomes. The true measure of your hard work is the personal awareness that you have worked to the best of your ability to complete a goal.

~~~

Use your Success Script to go out into the world and discover how the value you offer is best delivered. Your life and work will be more rewarding and much more fun.

● ● ●

Kim was trying to find a way to expand her business of home organizing. She had clients, but she was spending too much time servicing them—she wanted to discover a way to grow her business while spending less time with each client.

Using her Success Script, she stated the name of her business and her Instant Impact Message, "Get Organized Now: Creative organizing solutions for the home and office." Then she presented her two top services, "You can purchase this benefit by hiring me as an hourly consultant or by buying a three-month organizing package that includes my consulting time and onsite help."

To find a solution to her challenge, she asked for help. "Do you know of another way I can offer my services while spending less of my personal time delivering them?"

One of her current clients suggested that she form an organizing team to attack large projects, such as basements, garages, and closets. Kim loved the idea and formed a third service called "Team Organize!" that employed junior organizers to help sort, throw out, and organize large messes.

In less than a month, she wrote to me, "Team Organize! is going gangbusters. May was a record-breaking month—more than double an average month and significantly higher than my previous record. Working with my Success Script is probably the single most productive thing I spent my time on this year!"

● ● ●

STEP FOUR

Triumph by Becoming Inter"ask"ive

Action: Create your own luck by taking action every day.

Success: Acquiring the tools and ideas necessary to stick to and achieve your big dreams.

Now is the time to take action and make your goal a reality. Most people worry that "people will think I am full of myself if I talk big." Passion has grounded you, allowing you to confidently converse—a key to success. If you don't speak about your goal, no one can help you achieve success.

~~~

We are taught that reality destroys dreams. In fact, reality is the only thing that supports them.

~~~

You are capable of accomplishing your dream in a way that no one else can or has so far thought of. Starting a conversation with your Success Script enables people to understand and buy into your success. It also allows you to ask people specific questions about overcoming any challenges you may face—helping you obtain the resources, strategies, and contacts you need to succeed.

Start by recognizing possibilities in everything you do and in every person you meet. The more you practice discovering opportunities, the more they appear in your life.

~~~

Always be on your own path, not the path other people or society think you should follow.

~~~

Become Inter"ask"ive with a Question of the Day

We have to tell others about our goals in order to succeed. The secret to networking with confidence is to become *inter"ask"ive:* State your goal using your Success Script, and near the end of the conversation always ask a specific question that you feel you need answered.

〜〜

Tell others about your goal! No one knows
everything that needs to be completed or
wants to spend every waking moment gathering the resources and contacts required to
succeed. Turn your thoughts from, "What can I
do to achieve success?" to "How can I inspire
other people to help me achieve my goal?"

〜〜

Being inter"ask"ive takes practice. We have been ac-
customed to discovering information on our own rather
than asking for help.

〜〜

People love to feel smart—let them share their
secrets to success or refer you to someone
else who can provide the answers you need.

〜〜

Respect the amount of time people have to help you.
Be specific with your requests by setting a "question of
the day" every morning. This question defines the greatest challenge facing you right now. What single obstacle
do you need to overcome, no matter how large or small,
to catapult your goal forward?

Tim, who was looking to move from television development to production, made his question of the day, "Do

you know a team in the development area of our company that has a need for a financial expert?" Kim, the professional organizer growing her team, asked, "Do you know any professional women who would enjoy learning how to help others become more organized?"

Throughout the day, use your Success Script to establish a foundation for conversations. Then put out your specific question to others and listen to their ideas on how you can best overcome the challenge you are now facing.

Continually Discover Information

Do not stop asking your question once someone gives you a referral or answer—continue to solicit responses. You never know who will actually help you or what other unique strategies you will uncover that can move you forward faster.

Never let on how much you know about a subject. It causes the informer to censor himself. Invaluable pieces of information might be lost.

If you want to find a cheaper way to manufacture your product, share your Success Script with your colleagues and ask, "Do you know of anyone who can put me in touch with a cost-effective manufacturer?" If you want to find a date, ask your friends, "Do you know anyone who is single and would like to learn to appreciate art?"

Being specific in your requests allows people to refer others to you who can help you. Do not feel overwhelmed by the amount of information you receive. Just write it all down and decide later which items you will act on.

<center>~~~</center>

Recognize that a "Community of Opportunity" surrounds you—a supportive environment that continually provides you with the information you need to succeed.

<center>~~~</center>

Instead of setting a goal and becoming frustrated because you are not sure of what to do next, use the *question-of-the-day* technique to discover practical action steps you can take. Introduce yourself to others using your Success Script and ask, "What action steps would you take to overcome (*your current challenge*)?"

After you complete a step, examine what you have learned and decide the next logical step you should take. If you are unsure, just make the discovery of your next step your next question of the day.

State your first question of the day: _____

_____

_____

Become Open to Suggestions

Success is not a solo project; to move forward, you need the help of others. Slow down and get to know the people you meet. Their insights make the path toward achieving your dream shorter—even if it is as simple as a referral to people or resources to make your course more direct.

Taking action is better than waiting, even if it's just a small step toward success.

Provide the space people need to respond to your request. It is hard for some people to offer suggestions because more often than not, others judge and reject their ideas. Shift your mind into download mode by reclassifying suggestions as opportunities. Listen to all of the possibilities. Later, you can craft your chosen option into a unique solution.

Being open to suggestions creates self-confidence in your own experience and ideas. When you face future challenges, your mind automatically develops alternative solutions.

Becoming inter"ask"ive and open to ideas others present:

- Increases your confidence when speaking with others, because it gives you a practical way to start a conversation.

- Enables people to refer you to others who can help, because you asked a specific question that can and should be answered.

- Stimulates people's brains to provide you with contacts, resources, and strategies that will move your goal forward.

- Provides endless opportunities for you to create *your path* to success.

Do More Than the Expected!

Truly successful people find a unique approach to accomplishing their goals. They investigate and understand how others have previously achieved success, and then they confidently go beyond what is expected. They create a new path, *their own path,* to achieve success as they define it.

Learn by taking specific action toward accomplishing your goal and modifying your

path to success as you discover unique ways
to succeed.

For example, as a speaker at a national conference, I
asked the crowd:

- "How many of you came to this event to meet people?" The whole group raised their hands.
- "How many of you attended this event to learn something or gain contacts?" Again, everyone raised a hand.

I looked out at the crowd and said, "Both of those outcomes are given. You are told that if you attend networking
events you will meet people, learn something, and create
success. You assume that things will happen because you
are completing what everyone says are *the right actions.*

"Unfortunately, success is not automatic. You have to
work at making powerful connections with others. To
help you, people need to understand the benefit you
offer and the challenges you face."

To take less time creating success, don't just net-
work—discover ways to contact and connect with the
right people. Instead of just attending an event, partici-
pate in the event by using your Success Script, asking
your specific question of the day, and discovering the next
action step you can take toward success. You will be
amazed at how quickly other people support your progress forward.

～～～

I wanted to become a successful columnist, but I wasn't sure how I could make it a reality. Following the question-of-the-day process, I used my Success Script to introduce myself and listed "national columnist" as my third delivery method. Then I would simply ask, "Do you know anyone who can help make my Kick Start column a reality?" People gave me wonderful contacts—but I didn't stop asking for ideas until I had signed a deal. In three months, I had two columns in national magazines.

～～～

Constantly look for opportunities. Instead of watching television for the sake of entertainment, state your greatest challenge and see if the show you are watching can help you find a solution. You will be amazed at the actions characters take to overcome problems they face and how this new knowledge applies to your own life.

～～～

Intuitive people are never undecided. They go boldly forward knowing they are on the right path.

～～～

State one unusual action you can take to move your
goal forward:

_____

_____

_____

_____

_____

_____

Set Your Goal and Let It Blossom

Investigate alternatives. By focusing on the benefit that
you provide in your Instant Impact Message, you are exploring what is possible—not something that is tied to a
specific outcome or a process. Far more often than not,
when you push for something in life, a different result
than you expected arises.

Your mind makes up stories that may or may not be
true. Often, the negative outcomes we subconsciously
develop stop us from moving forward. Recognize when
these personal conversations occur and tell yourself,
"That's a possible outcome, but it most likely won't happen if I find the right information. I need to take action
and discover the truth."

Discover an answer, figure out how it applies to your
goal, and then let it go. It will open a space where you

can receive new answers. Don't force outcomes; there are too many good things that could happen.

❧

Through nonattachment, unexpected opportunities will come pouring forth. How much
fun is that?

❧

When you focus on a single way to accomplish a goal, you often miss all the other opportunities that surround you. Open yourself to new possibilities by recognizing that there are multiple paths to achieving your goals.

Start by defining just the first two steps you need to take to achieve your goal. Implement them. Then, let go of perceived limitations and (*this is important*) decide on your next right action. Create your unique path to achieving success by taking it.

❧

You can discover opportunities in everything
you do—whether it is a new product idea
while watching television or a new place to
take a date while shopping.

❧

Life on Your Terms

Goal setting also applies to creating a "To Do" list. To some people these lists seem magical: Record your next actions and you will achieve success. This belief sets up many people for failure. If they don't complete all the items on the list, they somehow think they are not serious about accomplishing their goals. However, completing an item that is not on the list may be the key to greater success.

To succeed with less frustration, continually follow through on your commitments. Time spent worrying is time squandered. Complete each task before moving on to something new. If a particular undertaking is frustrating to you, write down the next step you need to take and then take a break. When you return to a task, you can quickly revive your momentum.

Be bold in the actions you take. You have the ability to make the right decisions based on your intuition, heart, and the information you have gathered. Take a step forward, learn and then decide the next best action to take. Believe in yourself, and others will, too.

～～～

Use a To Do list if it works for you, but don't let it control your feelings or actions toward your success.

～～～

Engage Naysayers!

Negative comments have the power to crush ideas before they are even born. As you go after your goal, no matter how much success you have achieved in the past, when someone says something negative about your idea, or your abilities, it stings. Conventional wisdom says that: to succeed, you should follow your heart and ignore these naysayers.

Success comes from doing just the opposite. Your mission is to engage naysayers!

Some of the best ideas are born from unwelcome criticism. Negative comments have kernels of truth in them—people just don't always know how to correctly or constructively deliver messages. As you become more inter"ask"ive, your goal is to determine the truth beneath their comments and discover new information that will help you succeed.

~~~

People are here to help you, they are just uncertain how to do it. Engage them and discover new paths to success.

~~~

Listening to naysayers is especially important, because in most people's lives, including my own, the naysayers are family and people you love. Your spouse, friends, and family want you to succeed; however, they also want to protect you from the unknown and things that may be difficult.

Engaging loved ones when they become naysayers is especially difficult. They believe that if you develop answers to the questions before you start, you will be better prepared and therefore avoid unnecessary pain. Realize that behind each of their questions lies the subliminal message, "We love you and don't want to see you suffer!"

What loved ones fail to realize is how unhappy we may be in our current situations. Their caring for us actually prolongs our suffering. Instead of being frustrated, put a halt to these questions by engaging these people in your goal.

~~~

Your positive attitude will move other people into action. Very soon, like the common cold, everyone will catch success.

~~~

What naysayers say is a reflection of them, not you. Make naysayers important success allies by:

1. *Asking for their advice.* When someone says something negative, repeat back his or her statement and say, "You are right. Achieving success is hard. How

would you make it possible?" When you listen, their
defenses fall, and their years of experience come
pouring out. If they don't have an answer, they may
provide you with contacts who can help you succeed.

A client was creating a new toy for children. His
friend reminded him, "Well, have you talked to the
Consumer Product Safety Commission about safety
issues?" My client's subconscious immediately went
on the defensive, "What? What was that about? I am
just starting out on my idea."

Naysayers know more than you think. By simply
replying back, "Great idea, do you know anyone at
the commission so I can get specific information?"
He received some great information on product
safety requirements.

2. *Demonstrating that you want to hear their ideas.*
   Naysayers are used to people dismissing them rather
   than listening to their ideas. Be sympathetic to this,
   and give them an opportunity to respond. It's not
   helpful to try to persuade a naysayer that you are
   right, because it makes him defensive. Your goal is
   simply to find the truth in whatever he is saying.

3. *Complimenting them on their suggestions.* The easiest
   way to turn naysayers into allies is to make them feel
   appreciated. Be sincere about what you have learned
   from them. It's a rare occurrence for naturally negative types to be complimented. By doing so, you keep

their wheels spinning, and they may actually develop a solution to your most vexing problems.

~~~

Form the habit of giving attention to every thought and word of advice, even if they are negative. You will soon realize their importance.

~~~

List the top three things you think naysayers will say. Rather than ignoring them, create a response to engage these people in a conversation:

1. _____

2. _____

3. _____

Contact—Learn—Achieve
Success on Your Terms

If you are stuck, step outside of what you know. People are there to help; you just need to ask. Allow them to teach you how to achieve success. Call a person whose opinion you trust and seek simple advice by asking: "What is one thing I can do right now to move my goal forward?"

They may offer something as uncomplicated as asking your human resource department for open opportunities, calling one of their contacts, or sending an e-mail to your friends and family. Other people are free from the burdens you place on yourself and, therefore, can easily recognize opportunities that may be right in front of you.

Eliminate any notion that to achieve success you must "go it alone." Asking for help provides you with options you can explore, implement, and gain benefit.

Approach your intelligence gathering as if you are a reporter. You want to uncover new information that you can share with your audience to inspire them to read more. Do not judge or dismiss any ideas you receive. Circumstances change and what seems like a silly idea today may seem like inspired genius tomorrow.

Engaging other people in your goal helps you develop a strong belief in self—allowing a new direction and empowerment to arise. Connect with them by always stating ways they can further their success, not just how they can help you.

Others look at the world differently than you do and provide you with new insights and strategies for success.

Obtain a peek behind closed doors and notice how things really work. Charge forward by conducting research field trips and becoming inter"ask"ive with people who have achieved success, experts in your neighborhood, friends, family, and colleagues.

People Who Have Achieved Success

Learn from people who have achieved success by speaking with them and asking them questions about the challenges you face. Their personal experiences can reveal shortcuts you can take to create success.

Do not necessarily apply their ideas directly to your goal. Circumstances change; what worked for others in the past may not work for you. Discover tips that can help you succeed. Then use your intuition to modify them to fit with your goal, style, and personality.

If you don't have personal access to successful people, go to the library and read a biography of a person in your field who has achieved fame. You will be able to discover the action steps he or she took, laying a foundation for your own discovery. And soon, people will be asking you how they too can achieve their dreams.

List two successful people from whom you want to learn:

1. _____

2. _____

Experts in Your Neighborhood

Do not be too selective with people whom you speak to about your goals—you will miss amazing opportunities. The steps and strategies a person needs and uses to succeed in one area can be applied to additional areas of life.

Get to appointments early. Observe stores, restaurants, and parks around the place you are meeting. Paying careful attention to what is around you allows you to join in a personal conversation with the people you are meeting with—creating a solid foundation for success.

Successful neighbors of yours have had to overcome a variety of obstacles in order to achieve their goals. Be ready to introduce yourself first, people do not always have the confidence to say hello. If someone is promoted, starts a new business, or begins dating someone new, congratulate and learn from them.

Visit your neighborhood stores and, in addition to purchasing something, start up a conversation with the owners. Use your Success Script to tell them about your goal, ask them your "question of the day" and listen to their suggestions.

Storeowners' experiences apply to getting a job, starting a business, and inspiring others. You can discuss topics such as hiring people, dealing with customers, and juggling different roles.

An unexpected side benefit: Local storeowners probably know your neighbors better than you do; they can introduce you to others who can help you achieve success.

List two storeowners you will contact in the next week:

1. _____

2. _____

Friends, Family, and Colleagues

Don't let the personal side of achieving your goals make you crazy. Those closest to you are there to help but usually do not know how. Your question of the day is perfect to share with them—it explains your goal and gives them a specific task to work on.

Instead of just working on your goals, continually ask yourself, "Whom can I ask for help?" Success lies in DISCOVERY!!!!

Criticism from people we care about cuts a bit deeper. It takes a special focus to actually hear what they are saying rather than the tone they are using. Make the extra effort to understand their point and find something valid.

List two friends, family, or colleagues to share your goal and challenges with:

1. _____

2. _____

The Library

I am not sending you to the library for books; they are great resources but they take time to go through, I am sending you there to find articles related to your goal so you can obtain real-life information fast.

How does article research help you achieve success? Ask yourself, "What is a reporter's job?"

A reporter's job is to investigate and uncover unique ideas, strategies, and methods to achieving success. They report on new marketing trends, product ideas, time-saving techniques, corporate challenges, and much more. Use this information to find answers to the questions you have—saving yourself time, money, and frustration.

Moreover, people love to be quoted in articles. So, if you are looking for a person to contact at an organization (especially for a new job or to make a sale), you can find his or her name by researching pertinent articles.

You can find these articles in the library's free stacks of magazines or by logging onto its resource computer.

Input key words that are related to your goal ("jewelry design" "new jobs at Microsoft") into the computer. Magazine and newspaper articles that contain these key words are retrieved from their databases.

Remember, to achieve your goal faster, always ask for help. Introduce yourself using your Success Script and tell the librarian, "The Kick Start Guy told me about a computer system that helps me search through magazine and newspaper articles. Can you show me where it is and how I can use it?"

The librarian will show you how to use it and even suggest key words that you can input. Librarians are willing to teach and have years of experience, access them.

List the date you will visit the library:_____

Dream Like a Child, Decide As an Adult, and Go for It!

Life is not going to be perfect every day—problems are going to occur. It is important to develop the trust in yourself to take action based on your intuition. We cannot wait for certainty and the assurance that everything will work out as we would like it to. We must take risks if we are to live out our dreams.

When challenges appear, remember what your Grumble Buddy would say and ask yourself,

"That's nice, what am I going to do next?" And
do it!

Take a moment to answer these questions: Right now, could you make a living by singing? How about dancing? Right now, could you make a living by acting?

How did you answer? If you are similar to most people, you probably said "No" to all three.

Answer this last question: "If I had asked you these questions (Make a living dancing? Singing? Acting?) when you were five years old, what would you have said?"

"Yes! Of course!" is probably echoing throughout your mind.

Did you feel the possibilities and positive energy when you said yes? To discover new ways to achieve your goal with confidence, I ask you to wake up each morning and "Dream Like a Child, Decide As an Adult."

Adulthood does not mean you have to leave childhood behind. Dream like a child—open your mind and heart to discovering what is possible. Like a child, seek possibilities rather than obstacles. And ask for help when you need it.

Then, as an adult, use your intuition, your heart, and your knowledge to decide on the best action to take. Just say, "What can I do next to achieve my goal?"—and then trust your intuition and go do it!

〜〜

Expectancy always wins. Seek solutions rather than dismissing things as impossible, you will be surprised at what you discover.

〜〜

We often view the path to success as "all or nothing," which can intimidate us and stop us from moving forward. To relieve frustration, focus on progress not perfection. Conduct uncomplicated activities that will help you gain the knowledge and contacts you need. Every step you take is like a minireward. Thank yourself for accomplishing it, and take your next step. Intent, passion, and action will help you discover how to make your goal a reality.

The Oh, So Dreaded Double No

We all want to receive a "yes" whenever we request a favor or a specific action. Whether we are pitching a new idea, seeking approval from our boss, or making a simple change in the way we run our lives. Accomplishing something new is scary. Negative thoughts swim around in our minds, tiring our brain with unnecessary activity.

What if they don't like my idea? What if they don't believe I can accomplish it? And the hardest question of all: What if they say no?

~~~

Your life, career, and business are not marred by the number of No's you hear but they can dramatically improve with just one "Yes."

~~~

Some people fear asking for something again when they receive their first "no." This is normal. Fear is not something that you conquer—it is and always will be part of our experiences. *Fear provides the energy we need to achieve the impossible.*

Successful people embrace that energy; it is power ful. Apprehension soon subsides as you learn to *work with your fear* by not projecting "what might happen" and staying present to the possibilities. Keep moving forward by being inter"ask"ive and going for a "double no" by getting the person you request something from to deny you twice:

- *Go for "Yes."* You are capable and deserving of receiving a "yes" for any request you make. Establish a firm foundation for your goal by finalizing your Success Script. Listen to how people have accomplished your goal in the past, research current strategies, and develop the support materials you need. Then, create your own path to success that fits with your personality, and take action toward getting a "yes."

- *Treat every "no" as a maybe.* People do not always know how to communicate their intentions. And, we often read extra meaning into people's responses—treating a "not at this time" as a "no." In reality, the person may be preoccupied with a current commitment, completing a report, finishing a conversation, or just wanting to get out of the office and head home. Acknowledge the "no" but treat it as a "maybe." This simple act increases your energy.

- *Achieve the dreaded "double no."* After your first "no," reinvestigate how achieving your goal benefits the other person. Ignore the "no" you received, state three real-world contributions that achieving your goal will produce and ask again. For instance, emphasize how a new job will help your potential new boss solve a current challenge or how your new product fits in with his or her distribution plans. The worst that can happen is that the person repeats his or her "no."

- *Be positively relentless.* Some cultures tell us that going forward in the face of a "no" is a sign of weakness—a lack of applicable skills to achieve our goals. You are providing a unique benefit; always ask for help whether a positive or negative response occurs. Simply ask, "Do you know anyone else who can help support my goal?"

Michael went for a "double no" when he was buying a new car. After the salesman said "no" to the price Michael wanted to pay, he asked to speak to a manager. Acknowledging the benefits of a sale, he stated, "I researched new car prices and know that at this price your company makes money. My purchase adds to your monthly sales total and bonus, and I will help promote your dealership by telling my friends about your great service." He got the deal he sought.

~~~

Don't get discouraged if you are turned down. Keep going and believe in yourself and your goal—you will find individuals who will support your efforts.

~~~

Establish a Firm Foundation: Hold a Kick Start Success Launch Party

People are here to help; they just don't always understand how they can. It is important for those who surround you, especially friends and family, to understand your goal so they can support, rather than question your efforts. A great way for them to become informed of what you are trying to achieve is for you to hold a *Kick Start Success Launch Party.*

~~~

The emotional support you gain from friends and family can provide the unshakeable confidence you need to speak to others about your goal.

~~~

A Kick Start Success Launch Party is a gathering of people who are important in your life. During the party, they hear your Success Script and then brainstorm on ways to make your goal a reality. Do not analyze or judge any ideas that are presented, just write them down. You are in charge of your future. After everyone has left, you can decide which ideas you want to implement.

This gathering allows the people surrounding you to understand and support what you are trying to achieve.

To create a wonderful launch party:

- *Invite four to six friends and family members to your home for a Kick Start Success Launch Party.* Tell them that you are working on something very important to you, and you would love to hear their ideas on how you can create a unique success strategy. You will feed them and give them drinks. All they have to bring are their minds, bodies, and hearts.

- *Use your Success Script to introduce yourself and your goal.* Start the party by announcing your Success Script so that people understand your goal, the benefit you offer, and your passion for making it a reality. If anyone has questions, answer them to the best of your ability. If you do not know an answer, simply tell them, "That is a great question, and I am hoping to discover an answer to that as I take action to achieve my goal."

- *State your current challenge and ask for help.* Let them know what you need help with in order to achieve your goal. Then ask the group for ideas. If you want to know the names of companies that could use the benefit you offer, ask everyone. If you need to understand how to distribute a new product, ask for ideas.

- *L-I-S-Ten.* The first four letters of listen are L-I-S-T. As people share ideas and strategies with you, do not analyze them. Just write the ideas down in your notebook. As people realize you are open to receiving ideas, they will share even more. Your goal is to generate as many ideas as you can—filling up a "dream junk drawer of ideas."

- *Thank everyone for coming.* Send thank-you cards to everyone who attended—people appreciate them. They also act as a reminder to your guests of the goal you are trying to achieve, which may generate even more ideas and support.

~~~

It is hard to resist commenting on people's thoughts. Train yourself to just listen and explore the flow of new ideas.

~~~

State the date you will hold your Kick Start Success Launch Party _____

Make a list of friends and family members you are going to invite to your party:

1. _____

2. _____

3. _____

5. _____

4. _____

6. _____

Energize Your Spirit: Form a Success Team

Very few people in the world consistently believe in us. More often than not, you are your only true motivator. Even so, success necessitates integrating the advice and experience of others to construct new approaches to solving everyday challenges.

This is the principle behind creating a Success Team. It helps you discover exceptional ways to navigate beyond your dreams and create incredible opportunities. Your team fuels your belief in yourself and your capacity to take practical action toward success.

~~~

Incredible power is unleashed and negativity released when people support each other. Success Teaming connects your private "Eureka!" moments to the real world.

~~~

Keep the purpose of your Success Team simple: to motivate and inspire each other to take the next action step toward success. Team members provide a sounding board for exploring ideas and strategies. They do not provide direct answers to solving personal issues. Only you have the capability of discovering how you can best achieve success.

~~~

Everyone has self-doubt. Other people often see greater potential in you than you see in yourself—give them the venue to help boost your confidence.

~~~

Your Success Team consists of three to four people. The particular industry they work in, the goals they are trying to achieve, their level of education, and their experience are irrelevant. What matters is their ability to listen and motivate without interfering.

Success Teams meet regularly to encourage everyone involved to keep working on their goals by:

- Celebrating recent successes.

- Maintaining focus by discussing your next goal.

- Kick starting action by asking about your next action steps.

- Providing contacts or resources that can expand your possibilities.

- Motivating by sharing their experiences and ideas.

- Stating, "Sounds great. Keep going!"

Success Teams discuss task-oriented challenges. It is not a complaint or therapy session. Team members never discuss frustrations and doubts—that is the role of your Grumble Buddy. Your goal is to get the motivation you need to resolve the nonstop issues that accompany your individual path to success.

~~~

Do not compare yourself to other members on your team; your goals, and the path required to achieve them, are distinct. Be open to the evolution of your dream and your new life.

~~~

The greatest result of participating in a Success Team is that everything you want to achieve seems possible. You gain clear focus on your current goal and take the time to think through your strategy to achieve success.

~~~

Your mind-set can make or break your success. Kick start your subconscious into nurturing your big dreams by becoming part of a Success Team.

~~~

To kick start a goal or boost your spirit, it often only takes another person saying, "You can do it!" Surrounding yourself with smart, innovative people crystallizes your vision. The contributions of your Success Team empower you to attain your goals far more efficiently than taking action alone.

Fit Your Team into Your Life

One of my clients played basketball every Sunday morning. He decided to ask a few of his teammates if they were interested in coming a half hour early to the game and creating a Success Team. To his surprise, six people agreed. Every Sunday they now celebrate their achievements, share their current goals, and encourage each other to continue forward—returning home energized and empowered to strive for even greater success.

Make a list of people you are going to invite to be part of your Success Team:

1. _____

2. _____

3. _____

4. _____

● ● ●

Laid Off? A Success Team to the Rescue!

Jake had a feeling that a significant career change was about to occur. His boss had scheduled time on his calendar to discuss a "personnel issue." He knew that he produced outstanding work but still wasn't sure if it was good or bad news.

At the appointed time, Jake's boss was the first to speak, "The company has been going through some tough economic times. Unfortunately, your position has been eliminated."

Jake's heart sank. He had worked so hard developing new sales channels and growing the business and yet he was being downsized.

"But there is good news—we love your work and have found you a new position creating marketing collateral for our New Markets sector."

Jake was not thrilled because the job did not utilize his full skill set, but at least he still had a job. Rather than running scared, accepting things for the way they were, or feeling remorseful—he asked himself, "How can I obtain what I need out of this situation while benefiting my company?"

Jake began to work on his Success Script. His goal became "to contribute better to my company by making it grow faster." His Instant Impact Message related to his passion of "increasing revenue by developing innovative market penetration strategies."

Then, he started thinking about how he could create a Success Team at work that would help him and his company achieve greater success. While researching the division's product areas, an idea occurred to him. What if he combined what could be considered "new" market areas into one team—leveraging the company's competencies and saving it money by creating new joint strategies?

Additionally, of course, Jake was the right person to run such a group.

He defined how his experience could help expand the market for each of the areas. On his first call with his new boss, he thanked her for the opportunity and then, without hesitation, launched into his Success Script. He spoke confidently because he knew the worst she could say was, "No thank you, we want you to take the job we offered."

Jake's new boss listened to his passion and experience. At the end, she replied, "You have really put some thought into this. I am a proponent of teamwork. Let me consider it over the weekend." On Monday, Jake gained the responsibility of managing all three of the areas they had discussed.

The unexpected occurs when you have a conversation about possibilities.

• • •

Accept That You Are on the Right Path

In the late 1500s, there was a group of artists, musicians, sculptors, and writers who called themselves "The Wanderers." The lack of a support system in their hometowns made it challenging for members to blaze new creative trails.

Creating a life you love is not about obtaining validation from others—it's about achieving your goals on your terms.

The Wanderers met once a year. During their time together, they didn't ask what each person had accomplished or how much money he or she had generated. They simply met, shared their secrets to success, and told each other, "No matter where you are, you are on the right path. Keep working toward your goals."

This statement kept the members motivated to take action—and change the world we live in today.

Let go of your old self. Let new energy fill you and every day you will achieve beyond what you can imagine.

I believe the most powerful thing we can do is support another person's goal without question or reservation. The confidence and ideas this personal support generates allows people to conquer what may seem like impossible challenges.

I am resurrecting The Wanderers. Once a year, we will meet to share our secrets to success. Feel free to e-mail me at Romanus@kickstartguy.com, and I will return your e-mail with information about the group and our next meeting.

Congratulations!!!!

You are now on your path to achieve success, as defined by you. Remember to *Dream Like a Child*—always seeing possibility—and *Decide As an Adult*—taking action based on your intuition, knowledge, and the advice of others.

Keep achieving your goals and continue inspiring others to succeed in the process. The *world* is waiting!!!!

INDEX

119

ABOUT THE AUTHOR

Reaching over two million visionaries and entrepreneurs monthly, Romanus Wolter is "The Kick Start Guy." As the Success Coach for *Entrepreneur* magazine, the author of the popular *Kick Start Your Dream Business* (Ten Speed Press), and cofounder of www.KickStartSuccess.com, he provides practical, proven action steps that close the gap between goals and success.

Romanus has inspired thousands of people to create unique strategies for success. His action steps apply to both a person's life and career, giving them the ability to make powerful choices. Romanus's work changes "I can't" to "I will!" to "I did it!"

An American raised in Taipei, Taiwan, Romanus witnessed the birth of a new economy. Factories, movie theaters, stores, and restaurants appeared on every corner. This metamorphosis sparked something—the realization that the imagination is limitless. Any idea can become a reality.

As a speaker and radio host, Romanus's accessible wisdom provides the security and confidence people need to capitalize on opportunities. Through consulting engagements in London, Hong Kong, and the United States, he learned what it takes for people to succeed regardless of their education or skill set.

Popular Author	*Kick Start Your Success* (John Wiley & Sons)
	Kick Start Your Dream Business (Ten Speed Press)
Success Coach	*Entrepreneur* magazine
Columnist/Feature Writer	"Countdown to Start-Up" *Entrepreneur,* back page *Be Your Own Boss, The Magazine for Working Women*
Radio Host	Monthly segment on the *Entrepreneur Magazine* Radio Show
Cofounder	KickStartSuccess.com Web Portal
Founder/Former Director	San Francisco Small Business Development Center
Voting Member	San Francisco Mayor's Small Business Loan Committee

Featured In	*Chicken Soup for the Entre-preneurial Soul* and *The Ultimate Guide to Network Marketing*
Speaker of the Year	Small Business Administration and Success Builders International
Contributor/ Profiled	*MSNBC*, the *San Francisco Chronicle, Business Week*, the *Chicago Tribune, Quicken .com, Bloomberg Television*, and more
Masters of Business Administration	International Business, The American University